ILLUSTRATED STORIES FROM CHURCH HISTORY

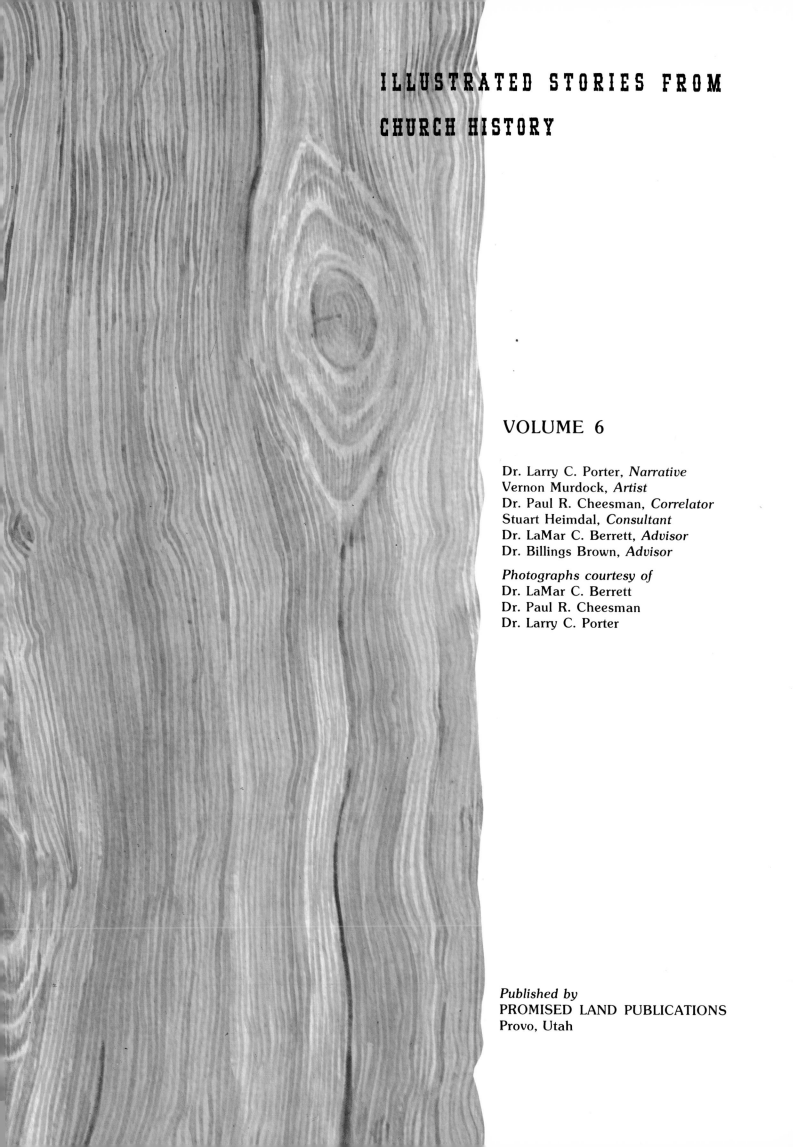

ILLUSTRATED STORIES FROM CHURCH HISTORY

VOLUME 6

Dr. Larry C. Porter, *Narrative*
Vernon Murdock, *Artist*
Dr. Paul R. Cheesman, *Correlator*
Stuart Heimdal, *Consultant*
Dr. LaMar C. Berrett, *Advisor*
Dr. Billings Brown, *Advisor*

Photographs courtesy of
Dr. LaMar C. Berrett
Dr. Paul R. Cheesman
Dr. Larry C. Porter

Published by
PROMISED LAND PUBLICATIONS
Provo, Utah

FIRST EDITION VOLUME 6, 1974

Lithographed in U.S.A.
PROMISED LAND PUBLICATIONS, INC.
Provo, Utah

CONTENTS

The capture of Far West... 8

"Majesty in chains".. 34

Imprisonment at Liberty Jail.. 42

A change of venue—escape!.. 64

Parley P. Pratt at Richmond and Columbia jails 66

Thousands flee Missouri 79

Fulfillment of Revelation by the Twelve.. 84

Illinois welcomes the Saints... 96

In search of a suitable location 102

"A day of miracles... 106

O God, where art thou? And where is the Pavilion that covereth thy hiding place?

How long shall thy hand be stayed, and thine eye, yea thy pure eye, behold from the eternal heavens the wrongs of thy people and of thy servants, and thine ear be penetrated with their cries?

Yea, O Lord, how long shall they suffer these wrongs and unlawful oppressions, before thine heart shall be softened toward them, and thy bowels be moved with compassion toward them?

O Lord God Almighty, maker of heaven, earth and seas, and of all things that in them are, and who controllest and subjectest the devil, and the dark and benighted dominion of Sheol—stretch forth thy hand; let thine eye pierce; let thy pavilion be taken up; let thy hiding place no longer be covered; let thine ear be inclined; let thine heart be softened, and thy bowels moved with compassion toward us.

Let thine anger be kindled against our enemies; and in the fury of thine heart, with thy sword avenge us of our wrongs.

Remember thy suffering saints, O our God; and thy servants will rejoice in thy name forever.

My son, peace be unto thy soul; thine adversity and thine afflictions shall be but a small moment;

And then, if thou endure it well, God shall exalt thee on high; thou shalt triumph over all thy foes.

Thy friends do stand by thee, and they shall hail thee again with warm hearts and friendly hands.

D&C, 121:1-9

CHAPTER VI

EXILES FROM MISSOURI

RESPONSIBILITY for carrying out Governor Lilburn W. Boggs' "Order of Extermination" was placed in the hands of General John B. Clark, commander of the First Division of the Missouri State Militia. However, other generals actually ended the Mormon War before Clark could arrive on the scene. Generals Samuel D. Lucas and David W. Atchison laid plans for an immediate march on Far West. On October 29, 1838, they moved their forces to a point sixteen miles south of the Mormon stronghold. The following day these troops were joined by General Alexander W. Doniphan who had already been operating in the area. On the outskirts of Far West, Doniphan's troops nearly cut off one hundred and fifty Mormon horsemen who had been patrolling the area south of the community. A member of Doniphan's command has given us a description of the lively action which followed:

> . . . we saw the Mormons under full run, aiming to beat us to town. Colonel Doniphan ordered us to charge and try to cut them off from town . . . . We all filed in after our leader, down the hill, across Goose Creek, in full speed . . . .
>
> The Mormons beat us, and had formed their line between us and town. We climbed the hill, formed our line right in front and not more than a hundred yards from them, awaiting orders, and expecting every moment to see the smoke and hear the report of their guns . . . .[1]

THE Mormons didn't choose to fire on the militia, however, as they wanted a peaceful settlement of the difficulties if possible. Nevertheless, the Prophet recognized the probability of a major battle and assembled the brethren on the public square at Far West. According to Ebenezer Robinson, Joseph "endeavoured to inspire the hearts of his hearers with courage, and deeds of valor, in defense of our families, our homes, and our firesides . . . ."[2]

11

WHEN the brethren observed the heavy concentration of militia moving against Far West, Brigham Young and Heber C. Kimball were appointed captains of fifty and commanded to take up positions on the direct route of the enemy into the town. Heber C. Kimball recalled this dangerous situation when he reported:

The army came up to within good rife-shot, and halted; seeing our temporary fortifications, which we had thrown up the night previous, by pulling down some of our houses, and fixing up our wagons; they dared not approach nearer, but retreated to Goose Creek, about three-fourths of a mile, screaming, hallooing and screeching; the devils in hell could not have made a more hideous howling. The mob declared there were fifteen hundred of us; but to my certain knowledge there were only about one hundred and fifty in that line.[3]

THE following day, Colonel George M. Hinkle, commander of the Mormon militia, attempted to negotiate with General Lucas. General Lucas provided him with a copy of Governor Boggs' "Order of Extermination" and delivered his own terms for a settlement of the war. His demands were as follows:

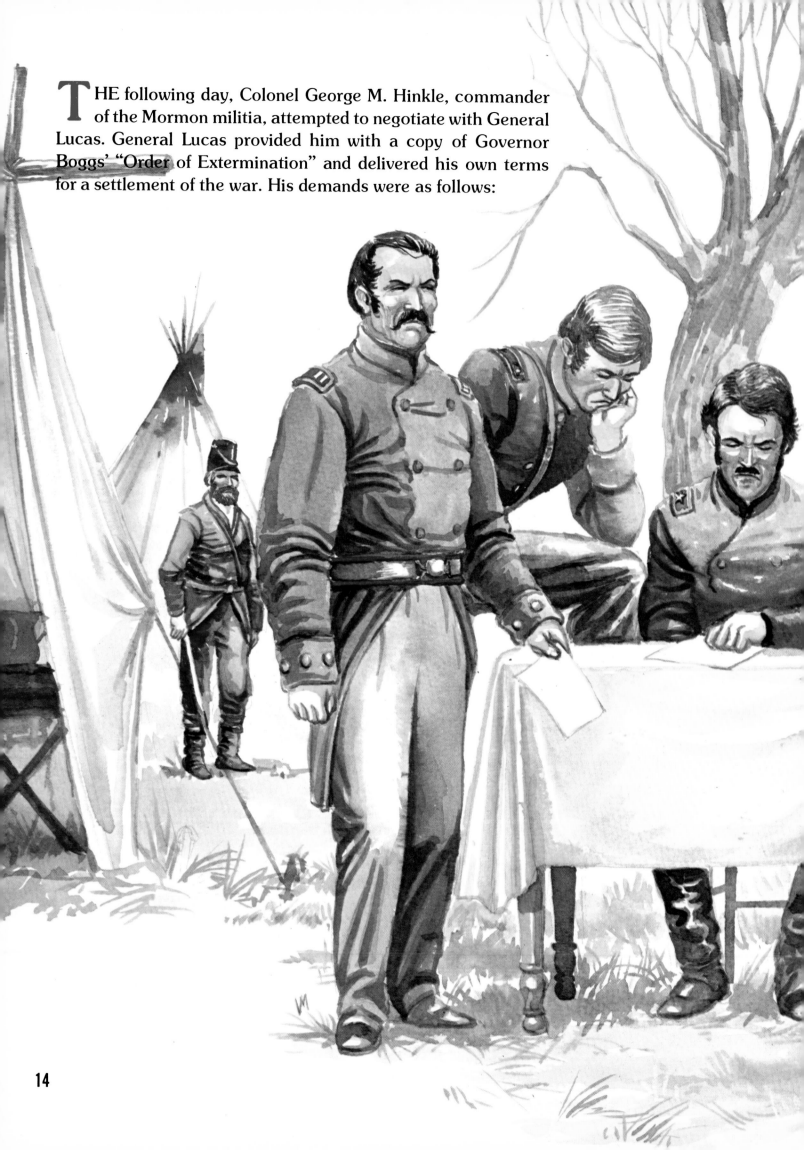

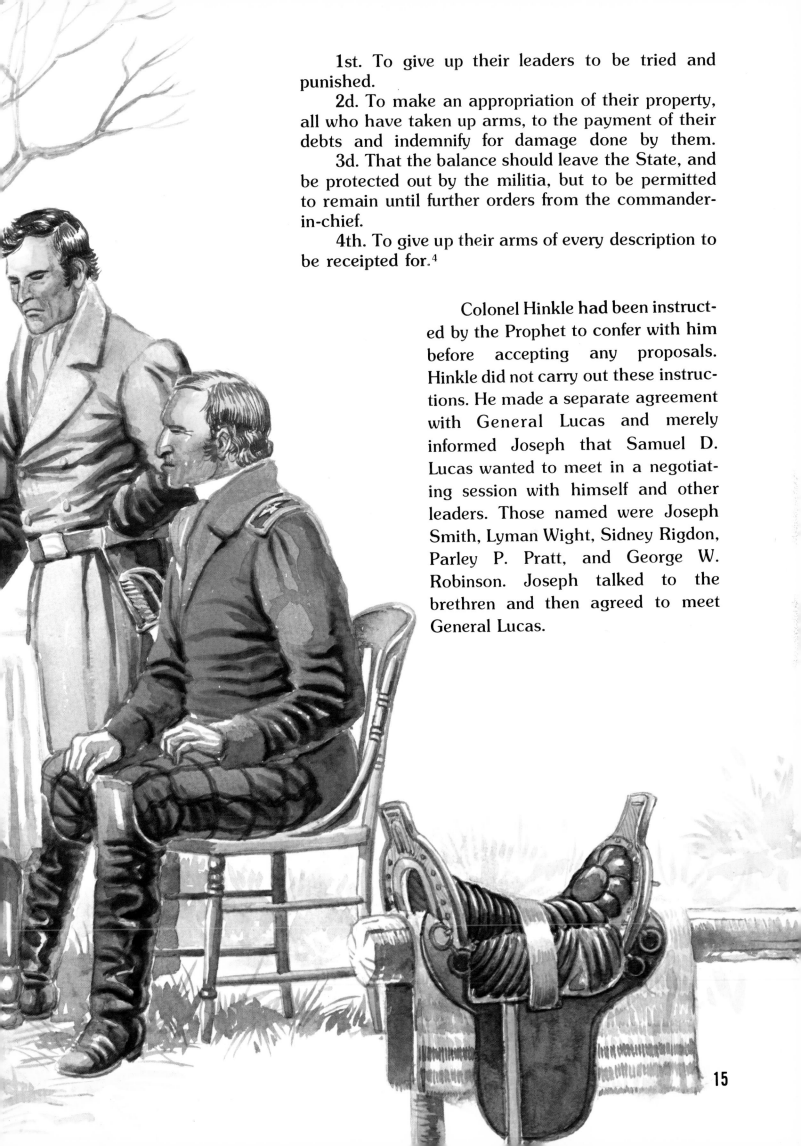

1st. To give up their leaders to be tried and punished.

2d. To make an appropriation of their property, all who have taken up arms, to the payment of their debts and indemnify for damage done by them.

3d. That the balance should leave the State, and be protected out by the militia, but to be permitted to remain until further orders from the commander-in-chief.

4th. To give up their arms of every description to be receipted for.[4]

Colonel Hinkle had been instructed by the Prophet to confer with him before accepting any proposals. Hinkle did not carry out these instructions. He made a separate agreement with General Lucas and merely informed Joseph that Samuel D. Lucas wanted to meet in a negotiating session with himself and other leaders. Those named were Joseph Smith, Lyman Wight, Sidney Rigdon, Parley P. Pratt, and George W. Robinson. Joseph talked to the brethren and then agreed to meet General Lucas.

15

AS the opposing parties met between the two lines, Colonel Hinkle suddenly exclaimed, "Here, general are the prisoners I agreed to deliver to you." General Lucas, who was mounted, immediately raised his sword and called, "You are my prisoners, and there is no time for talking at the present. You will march into the camp."[5] Parley P. Pratt has given us a vivid description of the scene that followed Lucas' command:

. . . we were marched into camp surrounded by thousands of savage looking beings, many of whom were dressed and painted like Indian warriors. These all set up a constant yell, like so many bloodhounds let loose upon their prey, as if they had achieved one of the most miraculous victories that ever graced the annals of the world . . .

In camp we were placed under a strong guard, and were without shelter during the night, lying on the ground in the open air, in the midst of a great rain. The guards during the whole night kept up a constant tirade of mockery, and the most obscene blackguardism and abuse. They blasphemed God; mocked Jesus Christ; swore the most dreadful oaths; taunted brother Joseph and others; demanded miracles, wanted signs, such as "Come, Mr. Smith, show us an angel." "Give us one of your revelations." "Show us a miracle." "Come there is one of your brethren here in camp whom we took prisoner yesterday in his own house, and knocked his brains out with his own rifle, which we found hanging over his fireplace; he lays speechless and crying; speak the word and heal him, and then we will all believe."[6]

WHILE the brethren were being mocked by their guards, General Lucas conducted a court-martial of the prisoners without their being allowed to be present. After a brief examination of their case, the court ordered that the captives be shot for their treasonous acts. General Lucas then issued this order:

Brigadier-General Doniphan:
Sir: — You will take Joseph Smith and the other prisoners into the public square of Far West and shoot them at 9 o'clock to-morrow morning.
SAMUEL D. LUCAS[7]

Alexander Doniphan openly refused to obey the order. In a written reply to his superior, Doniphan declared:

It is cold-blooded murder. I will not obey your order. My brigade shall march for liberty tomorrow at 8 o'clock; and if you execute these men, I will hold you responsible before an earthly tribunal, so help me God.
A.W. Doniphan
Brigadier-General[8]

Doniphan's prompt action saved the brethren from probable execution the following day. He was never called to account for his failure to obey a direct order although General Lucas did try to get Governor Boggs to remove Doniphan's military commission for his act of disobedience.[9] When Alexander W. Doniphan visited Salt Lake City in 1874, he was greeted by the Saints with much warmth. George A. Smith said of him on that occasion, "There are few men whose names have been identified with the history of our Church with more pleasant feelings to its members, than General Doniphan."[10]

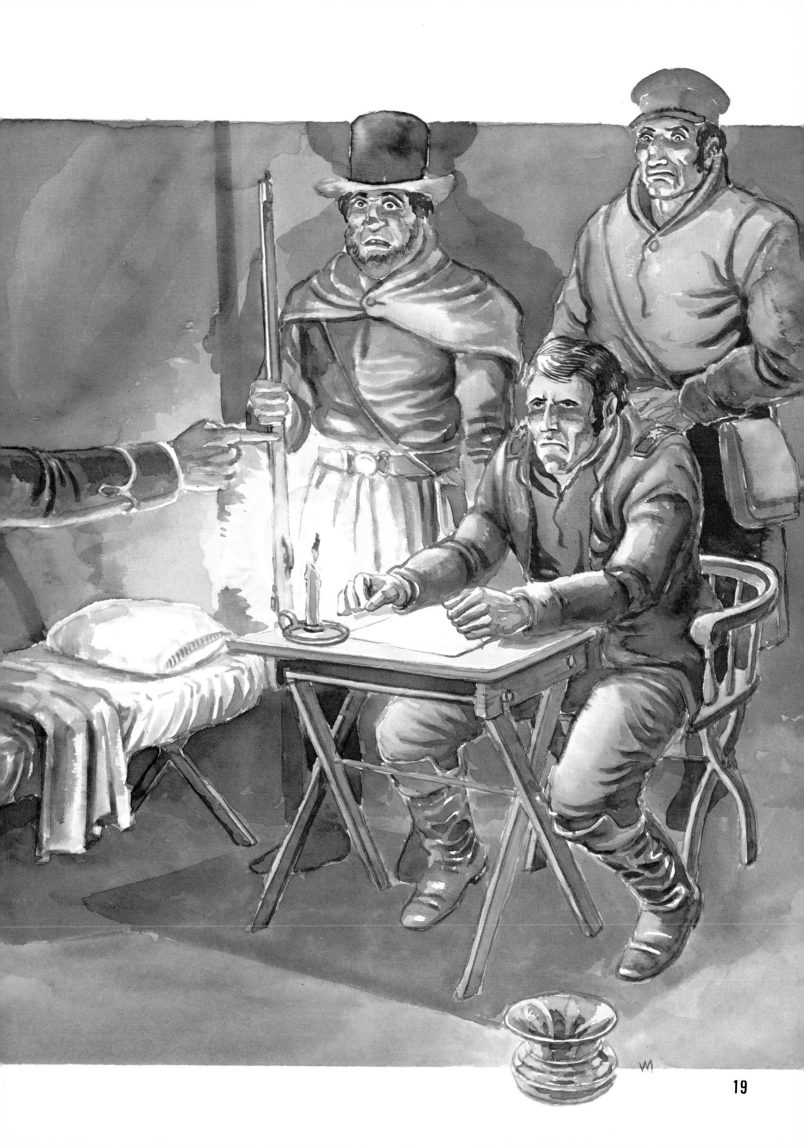

General Doniphan

THE next day, November 1, 1838, General Lucas ordered his troops to march to Far West for the formal surrender. His force formed a hollow square on the southeast side of the city. Colonel Hinkle marched the Far West militia into this square and directed them to ground their arms. He then rode forward and delivered up his sword and pistols to General Lucas.[11]

THE Missourians were especially anxious to capture and punish those Mormons who had fought against them in the Battle of Crooked River under Elder David W. Patten. However, they were dissappointed to learn that numbers of these brethren had gone into hiding or escaped the country. On the advice of Brigham Young, Samuel H. Smith, Charles C. Rich, Benjamin L. Clapp, Lorenzo D. Young and about twenty others had fled toward Illinois just before the capture of Far West. General Clark sent a company of fifty well armed men in hot pursuit with strict orders to bring the Mormons back either dead or alive. The Saints quickly sent a messenger to warn the escaping men of their dangerous situation. The moment the messenger arrived:

. . . a halt was called and Samuel asked what they should do in case the enemy overtook them; after a few moments' consultation the whole company covenanted with uplifted hands to heaven that if they were overtaken they would fight till they died, and not a man would fall into the hands of the enemy alive. They then traveled on ten miles and camped on the edge of some timber on the north side of a four mile prairie, and they afterwards learned that their enemies camped on the south edge of the same prairie, and would have overtaken them next day, had not the Lord sent a heavy snow storm during the night; and when the brethren arose in the morning, Phineas H. Young remarked, that that snow storm was their salvation. The air was so full of snow that they could hardly find their horses to saddle them, but they soon mounted them and continued their journey as fast as they could. The storm was from the north, and in their faces; it filled their tracks in a few moments, so that Clark's men could not follow.[12]

HEBER C. Kimball said that as soon as the Mormon defenders laid down their weapons at Far West, "The mob then commenced plundering the citizens of their bedding, clothing, money, wearing apparel, and everything of value they could lay their hands upon."[13]   A Mormon who had apostatized from the Church, William E. McLellin, came to where Heber was and chided him saying, "Brother Heber, what do you think of the fallen prophet now? Has he not led you blindfolded long enough? Look and see yourself, poor, your family stripped and robbed, and your brethren in the same fix; are you satisfied with Joseph?" Elder Kimball promptly replied:

Yes, I am more satisfied with him a hundred fold than ever I was before, for I see you in the very position that he foretold you would be in; a Judas to betray your brethren, if you did not forsake your . . . lying and abominations. Where are You? What are you about? You, and Hinkle, and scores of others; have you not betrayed Joseph and his brethren into the hands of the mob, as Judas did Jesus? Yes, verily, you have; I tell you Mormonism is true, and Joseph is a true prophet of the living God . . . .[14]

JOSEPH Smith and his fellow prisoners were marched from General Lucas' camp into the square at Far West. There the brethren were to be placed in a wagon and taken to Independence. Before leaving they successfully pleaded with their captors to allow them a moment to say goodby to their families. Joseph recorded this heart-rending separation:

I found my wife and children in tears, who feared we had been shot by those who had sworn to take our lives, and that they would see me no more. When I entered my house, they clung to my garments, their eyes streaming with tears, while mingled emotions of joy and sorrow were manifested in their countenances. I requested to have a private interview with them a few minutes, but this privilege was denied me by the guard. I was then obliged to take my departure. Who can realize the feelings which I experienced at that time, to be thus torn from my companion, and leave her surrounded with monsters in the shape of men, and my children, too, not knowing how their wants would be supplied; while I was to be taken far from them in order that my enemies might destroy me when they thought proper to do so. My partner wept, my children clung to me, until they were thrust from me by the swords of the guards. I felt overwhelmed while I witnessed the scene, and could only recommend them to the care of that God whose kindness had followed me to the present time, and who alone could protect them, and deliver me from the hands of my enemies, and restore me to my family.[15]

THE pain of separation from loved ones was again experienced by the Prophet and Hyrum as they, along with other prisoners, were placed in a wagon which was covered with canvas and the sides nailed down. General Moses Wilson and his brigade surrounded the vehicle, in readiness for the march to Jackson County. Just as they were about to depart, Joseph's mother and his sister, Lucy, were escorted through the throng to the wagon. Mother Smith described that tearful moment with her sons:

The man who led us through the crowd spoke to Hyrum, who was sitting in front, and, telling him that his mother had come to see him, requested that he should reach his hand to me. He did so, but I was not allowed to see him; the cover was of strong cloth, and nailed down so close, that he could barely get his hand through. We had merely shaken hands with him, when we were ordered away by the mob, who forbade any conversation between us, and, threatening to shoot us, they ordered the teamster to drive over us. Our friend then conducted us to the back part of the wagon, where Joseph sat, and said, 'Mr. Smith, your mother and sister are here, and wish to shake hands with you.' Joseph crowded his hand through between the cover and wagon, and we caught hold of it; but he spoke not to either of us, until I said, 'Joseph, do speak to your poor mother once more—I cannot bear to go till I hear your voice.' 'God bless you, mother!' he sobbed out. Then a cry was raised, and the wagon dashed off, tearing him from us just as Lucy pressed his hand to her lips, to bestow upon it a sister's last kiss—for he was then sentenced to be shot.[16]

AFTER camping for the night on Crooked River, the captives and their guards arose the next morning and made preparations to continue the ride to Independence. As they did so, Joseph spoke to the other prisoners in a cheerful and confidential tone, "Be of good cheer brethren; the word of the Lord came to me last night that our lives should be given us, and that whatever we may suffer during this captivity, not one of our lives should be taken."[17]

The prisoners were triumphantly exhibited to the people all along the road to Independence. As they entered Jackson County, some ladies and gentlemen visited the camp to see these strange followers. One of the women inquired of the troops which prisoner was the "Lord whom the 'Mormons' worshiped?" A guard pointed out the Prophet. Joseph narrated the conversation which followed, saying:

> The woman then turning to me inquired whether I professed to be the Lord and Savior? I replied, that I professed to be nothing but a man, and a minister of salvation, sent by Jesus Christ to preach the Gospel.
>
> This answer so surprised the woman that she began to inquire into our doctrine, and I preached a discourse, both to her and her companions, and to the wondering soldiers, who listened with almost breathless attention while I set forth the doctrine of faith in Jesus Christ, and repentance, and baptism for re-mission of sins, with the promise of the Holy Ghost, as recorded in the second chapter of the Acts of the Apostles.
>
> The woman was satisfied, and praised God in the hearing of the soldiers, and went away, praying that God would protect and deliver us.[18]

AT Independence a large crowd assembled to have a look at the prisoners. Joseph and his brethren were placed in a vacant house where they were required to sleep on the floor. They were later moved to the Knowlton Hotel and treated more kindly. Numbers of people flocked to see them and their time was spent in preaching and conversation. The brethren were even allowed to visit the temple lot and walk the streets of Independence. However, their stay in that community was shortened by the arrival of Colonel Sterling Price with orders from General Clark to General Lucas directing that the captives be brought to Richmond in Ray County. Parley P. Pratt recorded the circumstances of the transfer:

> Generals Lucas and Wilson had tried in vain to get a guard to accompany us; none would volunteer, and when drafted, they would not obey orders; for in truth, they wished us to go at liberty.

At last a colonel and two or three officers started with us, with their swords and pistols, which was more to protect us than to keep us from escaping. On this journey some of us rode in carriages, and some on horseback. Sometimes we were sixty or eighty rods in front or rear of our guard, who, by the by, were three sheets in the wind, in the whiskey line, having a bottle in their pockets; but knowing that we were not guilty of any crime, we did not wish to escape by flight. At night, having crossed the ferry, we put up at a private house. Here our guards all went to bed and to sleep, leaving us their pistols to defend ourselves in case of any attack from without, as we were in a very hostile neighborhood.[19]

IN Richmond the brethren were again imprisoned in an old vacant house, but this time their treatment was far from cordial. Joseph stated:

. . . Colonel Price came in with two chains in his hands, and a number of padlocks. The two chains he fastened together. He had with him ten men, armed, who stood at the time of these operations with a thumb on the cock of their guns. They first nailed down the windows, then came and ordered a man by the name of John Fulkerson, whom he had with him, to chain us together with chains and padlocks, being seven in number. After that he searched us, examining our pockets to see if we had any arms. He found nothing but pocket knives, but these he took away with him. [20]

COLONEL Price allowed the guards to torment and abuse the prisoners unmercifully. Foulmouthed and vulgar, these base men kept up a torrent of oaths and obscene jests directed at their Mormon captives. One night when this filthy language was at its height and the guards were recounting deeds of murder and robbery committed against the Saints, Parley P. Pratt could scarcely contain himself. He lay next to the Prophet and knew that he was awake and as troubled as himself. Suddenly Joseph was on his feet and in a voice of thunder exclaimed:

SILENCE, ye fiends of the infernal pit. In the name of Jesus Christ I rebuke you, and command you to be still; I will not live another minute and hear such language. Cease such talk, or you or I die THIS INSTANT! [21]

Elder Pratt expressed the singular effect of that moment on all the hearers:

> He [Joseph] ceased to speak. He stood erect in terrible majesty. Chained, and without a weapon; calm, unruffled and dignified as an angel, he looked upon the quailing guards, whose weapons were lowered or dropped to the ground; whose knees smote together, and who, shrinking into a corner, or crouching at his feet, begged his pardon, and remained quiet till a change of guards.
>
> I have seen ministers of justice, clothed in magisterial robes, and criminals arraigned before them, while life was suspended on a breath, in the Courts of England; I have witnessed a Congress in solemn session to give laws to nations; I have tried to conceive of kings, of royal courts, of thrones and crowns; and of emperors assembled to decide the fate of kingdoms; but dignity and majesty have I seen but once, as it stood in chains, at midnight, in a dungeon in an obscure village of Missouri. [22]

WHEN Joseph and his party first arrived in Richmond they found that some fifty-six of their brethren had been seized at Far West, by order of General Clark, and brought to Richmond before them. They were imprisoned in an unfinished brick courthouse which was then under construction. Most of these Saints were later released, but not before they had been subjected to many abuses.

General Clark maintained that Joseph and his fellow prisoners should be tried by court-martial and busily searched the military law to find the necessary authority to shoot the captives. Hyrum Smith recalled how close they came to death when he stated:

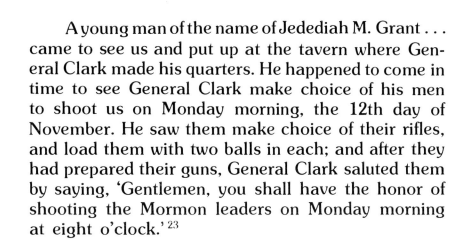

A young man of the name of Jedediah M. Grant . . . came to see us and put up at the tavern where General Clark made his quarters. He happened to come in time to see General Clark make choice of his men to shoot us on Monday morning, the 12th day of November. He saw them make choice of their rifles, and load them with two balls in each; and after they had prepared their guns, General Clark saluted them by saying, 'Gentlemen, you shall have the honor of shooting the Mormon leaders on Monday morning at eight o'clock.' [23]

RELUCTANTLY, General Clark was finally compelled to turn over his prisoners to the civil courts for trial. Before Judge Austin A. King, a legal hearing or court of inquiry was conducted to determine which of the prisoners might be committed to jail on the basis of the evidence submitted. Those held would appear before a grand jury for further action against them. The inquiry lasted from November 12 to 28, 1838. Alexander W. Doniphan and Amos Reese served as lawyers for the Saints. During the course of the inquiry, the brethren were indicted on charges of "high treason, and other crimes against that State."[24]

When the Mormons supplied the names of those witnesses they wished to have called for the defense, the court sent Captain Samuel Bogart to bring them in. However, Bogart either intimidated the witnesses so that they would not appear or cast them into prison. So desperate were the Saints to obtain a witness in their behalf that they actually summoned one brother right off the street. Parley P. Pratt testified:

A member of the Church, named Allen, was just then seen to pass the window. The prisoners requested that he might be introduced and sworn. He was immediately called in and sworn. He began to give his testimony, which went to establish the innocence of the prisoners, and to show the murders, robberies etc., committed by their accusers. But he was suddenly interrupted and cut short by cries of "Put him out;" "Kick him out;" . . . "shoot him;" "Kill him . . ."

The Court then ordered the guard to put him out, which was done amid the yells, threats, insults and violence of the mob who thronged in and around the court house. He barely escaped with his life. Mr. Doniphan, attorney for the defence, and since famed as a general in the Mexican war, finally advised the prisoners to offer no defence; "for," said he, "though a legion of angels from the opening heavens should declare your innocence, the Court and populace have decreed your destruction."[25]

JUST before the end of the hearing, a number of the brethren were released because nothing had been proven against them. At the conclusion of the inquiry, Parley P. Pratt, Morris Phelps, Luman Gibbs, Darwin Chase, and Norman Shearer were committed to prison there in Richmond. However, Joseph Smith, Hyrum Smith, Sidney Rigdon, Lyman Wight, Caleb Baldwin and Alexander McRae were sent to jail at Liberty in Clay County by decree of the court. Hyrum Smith said:

The next morning a large wagon drove up to the door, and a blacksmith came into the house with some chains and hand-cuffs. He said his orders were from the Judge to handcuff us and chain us together. He informed us that the Judge had made out a mittimus and sentenced us to jail for treason. He also said the Judge had done this that we might not get bail. He also said the Judge declared his intention to keep us in jail until all the "Mormons" were driven out of the state. He also said that the judge had further declared that if he let us out before the "Mormons" had left the state, we would not let them leave, and there would be another . . . fuss kicked up.

. . . the blacksmith proceeded and put the irons upon us, and we were ordered into the wagon, and drove off for Clay county.[26]

Liberty jail as it looked on Sept. 18, 1888. The three men are Andrew Jenson, Edward Stevenson and Joseph B. Black.

The L.D.S. visitor's center located on the site of the Liberty jail in Independence, Missouri.

THE journey from Richmond to Liberty was made in one day. Joseph and his fellow prisoners were again exhibited along the way to the local inhabitants. As they approached the jail house, a multitude of people gathered to witness the event. Among those in the crowd was a young Latter-day Saint, Lyman O. Littlefield. He wrote:

The prisoners left the wagon and immediately ascended the south steps to the platform, around which no banisters were constructed. The door was open, and one by one, the tall and well proportioned forms of the prisoners entered. The Prophet Joseph was the last of the number who lingered behind. He turned partly around, with a slow and dignified movement, and looked upon the multitude. Then turning away, and, lifting his hat, he said, in a distinct voice, "Good afternoon, gentlemen." The next moment he had passed out of sight. The heavy door swung upon its strong hinges and the Prophet was hid from the gaze of the curious populace who had so eagerly watched. [27]

A model cutaway of the interior of Liberty jail.

FROM the latter part of November 1838, to the forepart of April 1839, Liberty Jail was to be the Prophet's place of confinement. So that the reader might better understand the cramped quarters experienced by the brethren during almost five months of imprisonment, the following description is added:

The jail in which the prisoners in Liberty were housed was a structure composed of rock and wood. The walls were of double construction, the outer portion being stone and the inner oak-hewn logs. The space between the inner and outer walls of the building were filled with loose rock, making the total thickness of the walls about four feet in all.

The overall size of the structure was twenty-two feet in width by twenty-two feet in length by fourteen feet in height. The building was divided into two compartments, one above and one below. The upper story was just over seven feet from floor to ceiling and housed the jailer and his family, while the lower apartment or dungeon was just under six feet in height and was reserved exclusively for prisoners.

The dungeon chamber was smaller than the rest of the building, being only fourteen and one-half feet from east to west, inside dimensions, and fourteen feet from north to south. The ceiling of the dungeon was also made of logs. It was overlaid with several loads of rock to prevent escape through to the upper compartment.[28]

THE crowded conditions, insufficient heat and bad food created a long and difficult winter for Joseph and his fellow prisoners. In a letter, the Prophet described their sad situation when he said:

We are kept under a strong guard night and day, in a prison of double walls and doors, proscribed in our liberty of conscience, our food is scant, uniform, and coarse; we have not the privilege of cooking for ourselves, we have been compelled to sleep on the floor with straw, and not blankets sufficient to keep us warm; and when we have a fire, we are obliged to have almost constant smoke. The Judges have gravely told us from time to time that they knew we were innocent, and ought to be liberated, but they dare not administer the law unto us for fear of the mob. But if we deny our religion, we can be liberated.[29]

FORTUNATELY for the brethren, numerous friends visited them during their imprisonment and cheered their spirits. Commenting on these welcome moments, Alexander McRae later wrote:

Among our friends who visited us, were Presidents Brigham Young and Heber C. Kimball, . . . George A. Smith of the quorum of the Twelve; Don C. Smith, brother of Joseph, came several times, and brought some of our families to see us. Benjamin Covey, Bishop of the Twelfth Ward of this city, [Salt Lake] brought each of us a new pair of boots, and made us a present of them. James Sloan, his wife and daughter, came several times. Alanson Ripley also visited us, and many others, whom to name would be too tedious. Orin P. Rockwell brought us refreshments many times; and Jane Bleven and her daughter brought cakes, pies, etc., and handed them in at the window. These things helped us much, as our food was very coarse, and so filthy that we could not eat it until we were driven to it by hunger.[30]

WHILE confined in the dampness of Liberty Jail, Sidney Rigdon became ill with fever. At times he was left so weak that he couldn't stand. Mrs. George Robinson, Sidney's daughter, came into the county jail and nursed him during his sickness. In time, Elder Rigdon and the other brethren were finally able to secure an appearance in court. Sidney was extremely ill and therefore asked for a cot or bed to be placed in the court-room because he was too weak to sit in a chair. The room was filled with about one hundred "Mormon Eaters" who were greatly excited against the brethren. Alexander W. Doniphan, who acted as lawyer for the elders, was asked by Brother Rigdon if he couldn't plead his own case. Doniphan agreed to this and reported the proceedings when he said:

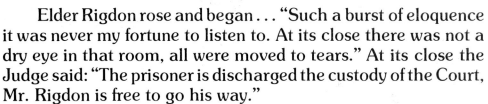

Elder Rigdon rose and began . . . "Such a burst of eloquence it was never my fortune to listen to. At its close there was not a dry eye in that room, all were moved to tears." At its close the Judge said: "The prisoner is discharged the custody of the Court, Mr. Rigdon is free to go his way."

The effect of Elder Rigdon's words was such that one of the leading men of the crowd picked up his hat, and turning to the bystanders, said, "We came here determined to do injury to this man. He is innocent of crime, as has been made to appear. And now gentlemen, out with your money and help the man to return to his destitute family." He circulated the hat and the money was showered into it till he placed a hundred dollars in Elder Rigdon's hands, with the remark, "Now old gentleman, make the quickest possible time to your family, who need you and your help."[31]

Sidney was admitted to bail, which meant that he would still have to stand trial at an appointed time. However, as it actually worked out, the sheriff gave him a pistol, a horse, and also provided a guide to take him where his family was waiting. The sheriff then told him to make his escape from the mob with all possible speed.[32] Tired of the injustices experienced in Missouri, Elder Rigdon followed directions and shortly thereafter fled to the State of Illinois. The brethren, including the Prophet, were returned to their cells, pending further hearings.

FRUSTRATED in their many attempts to get a fair and impartial trial, Joseph and his fellow prisoners made at least two attempts to escape from Liberty Jail. On the first occasion, the prisoners asked Joseph which night would be the best for the escape. He inquired of the Lord and then assured them that that very evening, February 7, 1839, was the time to go. However, Lyman Wight said that he would not make the attempt that evening, but would go with them if they waited until the next night. Even though they had no promise of success on the following evening, the brethren agreed to wait. The prisoners later regretted their decision. That first night, the conditions would have been perfect for their flight. Alexander McRae recorded the circumstances in these words:

> When night came, the jailer came alone with our supper, threw the door wide open, put our supper on the table, and went to the back part of the room, where a pile of books lay, took up a book, and went to reading, leaving us between him and the door, thereby giving us every chance to go if we had been ready. As the next day was agreed upon, we made no attempt to go that evening.

... unfortunately for us, the timber of the wall being very hard, our auger handles gave out, and hindered us longer than we expected; we applied to a friend, and a very slight incautious act gave rise to some suspiciouns, and before we could fully succeed, our plan was discovered; we had every thing in readiness, but the last stone, and we could have made our escape in one minute, and should have succeeded admirably, had it not been for a little imprudence or over-anxiety on the part of our friend. [34]

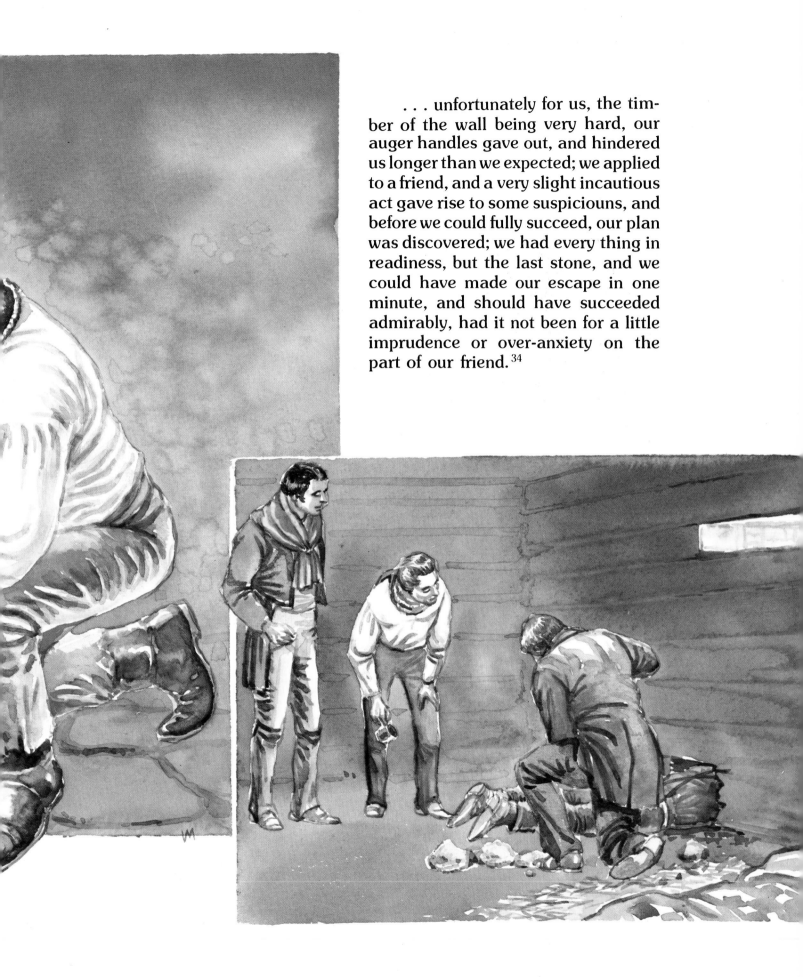

THE Prophet and other inmates wrote many letters to the
Saints and loved ones while held in Liberty Jail. Perhaps
the best known of these was an inspired revelation presently found
in the Doctrine and Covenants, Section 121. Joseph was filled
with sadness as he continued to witness the harsh treatment given
the Saints in Missouri. He had to stand helplessly by while his
people were driven from that State. In the anguish of his soul
he cried out:

O God, where art thou? And where is the pavilion that covereth thy hiding place?

How long shall thy hand be stayed, and thine eye, yea thy pure eye, behold from the eternal heavens the wrongs of thy people and of thy servants, and thine ear be penetrated with their cries.

Yea, O Lord, how long shall they suffer these wrongs and unlawful oppressions, before thine heart shall be softened toward them, and thy bowels be moved with compassion toward them?[35]

To Joseph's troubled heart, the Lord gave thoughtful and instructive comfort as he replied:

My son, peace be unto thy soul; thine adversity and thine afflictions shall be but a small moment;

And then, if thou endure it well, God shall exalt thee on high; thou shalt triumph over all thy foes.

Thy friends do stand by thee, and they shall hail thee again with warm hearts and friendly hands.[36]

THE Prophet was not then aware of just how quickly his friends would be greeting him "with warm hearts and friendly hands." Judge Austin A. King ordered the prisoners removed from Liberty Jail to Daviess County for trial. Joseph and the others were taken to Gallatin where, said the Prophet, "Our trial commenced before a drunken grand jury, Austin A. King, presiding judge, as drunk as the jury; for they were all drunk together."[37]   One of the witnesses examined for the defense was a faithful Saint, Elder Stephen Markham. The Prophet explained that Brother Markham nearly lost his life as a consequence. Joseph stated:

> Markham was permitted to give his testimony. After he had closed, Blakely, one of the guard, came in and said to Markham, that he wanted to speak to him. Brother Markham walked out with him, and around the end of the house when Blakely called out, "----- ----- you ----- old Mormon; I'll kill you;" and struck at Markham with his fist and then with a club. Markham took the club from him and threw it over the fence.

There were ten of the mob who immediately rushed upon Markham to kill him, Colonel William P. Penniston, captain of the guard, being one of the number. But Markham told them he could kill the whole of them at one blow apiece, and drove them off. The court and grand jury stood and saw the affray, and heard the mob threaten Markham's life, by all the oaths they could invent, but they took no cognizance of it.

The ten mobbers went home after their guns to shoot Markham, and the grand jury brought in a bill for "murder, treason, burglary, arson, larceny, theft, and stealing," against Lyman Wight, Alexander McRae, Caleb Baldwin, Hyrum Smith and myself.[38]

THAT night, the visions of the future were opened to the Prophet's understanding. He saw the near approach of his own escape from imprisonment and also the danger that his beloved friend, Stephen Markham was in. Joseph immediately awakened Brother Markham and told him that he must get up very early and not wait to talk to the judge and lawyers, as he had planned to do. If he did so he would get home safely. Markham arose at dawn and rode rapidly to Far West. The mob pursued with the idea of shooting him, but could not overtake the swift rider.[39]

SOON after their arrival in Gallatin, the brethren received word that they had been granted a change of venue (transferring the cause for trial to another county or district) from Daviess County to Columbia, Boone County, Missouri. Joseph's vision was about to be enacted — the moment for escape had come. Hyrum Smith has given us a detailed account of events leading to their freedom. As the prisoners and their guard left Gallatin, April 15, 1839, he said:

They fitted us out with a two-horse wagon, and horses, and four men, besides the sheriff, to be our guard. There were five of us. We started from Gallatin in the afternoon, the sun about two hours high, and went as far as Diahman that evening and stayed till morning. There we bought two horses of the guard, and paid for one of them in clothing, which we had with us; and for the other we gave our note.

We went down that day as far as Judge Morin's — a distance of some four or five miles. There we stayed until the next morning, when we started on our journey to Boone county, and traveled on the road about twenty miles distance. There . . . the sheriff showed us the mittimus before referred to, without date or signature, and said that Judge Birch told him never to carry us to Boone county, and never to show the mittimus; and, said he, I shall take a good drink of grog and go to bed, and you may do as you have a mind to.

Three others of the guard drank pretty freely of whisky, sweetened with honey. They also went to bed, and were soon asleep, and the other guard went along with us, and helped to saddle the horses.

Two of us mounted the horses, and the other three started on foot, and we took our change of venue for the state of Illinois, and in the course of nine or ten days arrived safe at Quincy, Adams county, where we found our families in a state of poverty, although in good health, they having been driven out of the state previously by the murderous militia, under the exterminating order of the executive of Missouri . . . [40]

PARLEY P. Pratt and the brethren imprisoned with him at Richmond, were not as fortunate as the Prophet in securing their release. Some nine months went by before they successfully escaped their persecutors. Within a few days of their initial arrest, almost all of those jailed with Parley were released on bail. Eventually, Darwin Chase and Norman Shearer were also released, leaving only Parley, Morris Phelps, King Follett and Luman Gibbs. Gibbs had denied the faith and turned traitor, but was retained in jail to spy on the brethren. For this he was treated very well and given many privileges.

After a long, dreary winter and spring in the prison at Richmond, these elders were also able to obtain a change of venue to Columbia, Boone County, Missouri. Sheriff Brown coupled the prisoners together with wrist irons and put them in a carriage. They were then surrounded by four armed guards on horseback. During the second day of their journey, Elder Pratt and his companions found themselves in a very dangerous situation. The rain was falling in torrents and darkness was setting in rapidly. Parley explained:

> Four miles of wild country, partly covered with forests and underwood, still lay between us and the nearest house. Through the hurry of the moment, or for some other reason, they neglected to replace our irons, and our limbs were free. The carriage drove through a thick forest during the extreme darkness, and was several times on the eve of upsetting. This caused us to assume a position for saving ourselves by rising upon our feet, ready to jump out in case of the carriage upsetting.

The Sheriff and guards seeing this, rode close on each side, and cocking their pistols, swore they would shoot us dead if we attempted to leave the carriage, and that if it upset they would shoot us anyhow, for fear we might attempt to escape.[41]

IN the forepart of July 1839, Orson Pratt, Mrs. Phelps and her brother, a Mr. Clark, came to see their relatives at Columbia Jail. During their visit, plans were laid for an attempted escape. Sundown, on the evening of the fourth of July was agreed upon. It was then that the door would be opened to hand in their evening meal. On the fourth, the prisoners and their company hid their anxieties by joining in the spirit of the national celebration. Parley related:

We had prevailed on the keeper to furnish us with a long pole, on which to suspend a flag, and also some red stripes of cloth. We then tore a shirt in pieces, and took the body of it for the ground work of a flag, forming with the red stripes of cloth an eagle and the word "Liberty," in large letters. This rude flag of red and white was suspended on the pole from the prison window, directly in front of the public square and court house, and composed one of the greatest attractions of the day. Hundreds of people from the country, as well as villagers who were there at the celebration, would come up and stare at the flag, and reading the motto, would go swearing or laughing away, exclaiming, "Liberty! Liberty! What have the Mormons to do with celebrating Liberty in a ------ old prison?"[42]

FOLLOWING the noon meal, Orson Pratt and Brother Clark left with a flurry of goodbyes and well wishes, as though they were on their way to Illinois. In reality, they merely rode out of town and then doubled back to a patch of woods just about a half mile from prison. With them were three horses for the escapees. All was in readiness, as indicated by Parley's narration:

> In this, as in most other fields of battle, where liberty and life depend on the issue, every one understood the part assigned to him and exactly filled it. Mr. Follett was to give the door a sudden pull, and fling it wide open the moment the key was turned. Mr. Phelps being well skilled in wrestling was to press out foremost, and come in contact with the jailer; I was to follow in the centre, and Mr. Follett, who held the door, was to bring up the rear, while sister Phelps was to pray.

> No sooner was the key turned than the door was seized by Mr. Follett with both hands; and with his foot placed against the wall, he soon opened a passage, which was in the same instant filled by Mr. Phelps, and followed by myself and Mr. Follett. The old Jailer strode across the way, and stretched out his arms like Bunyan's Apollion, or like the giant Despair in Doubting Castle, but all to no purpose. One or two leaps brought us to the bottom of the stairs, carrying the old gentleman with us headlong, helter skelter, while old Luman sat and laughed in his corner of the prison, and Mrs. Phelps exclaimed, "O Lord God of Israel, thou canst help." Old Mrs. Gibbs looked on in silent amazement, while the jailer's wife acted the part of the giant Despair's wife, Diffidence, and not only assisted in the scuffle, but cried out so loud that the town was soon alarmed. In the meantime we found ourselves in the open air, in front of the prison and in full view of the citizens, who had already commenced to rally, while Mr. Phelps and the jailer still clinched fast hold to each other like two mistaffs. However, in another instant he cleared himself, and we were all three scampering off through the fields towards the thicket.[43]

THE prisoners were closely pursued by "soldiers in uniform, mounted riflemen, footmen with fence stakes, clubs, or with whatever came to hand, and with boys, dogs, etc., all running, rushing, screaming, swearing, shouting, bawling and looking, while clouds of dust arose behind them."[44]   Parley leaped into the saddle and was taking about the third jump with his horse when a man pointed a rifle at his head and pulled the trigger. The cap on the weapon burst, but the powder wouldn't burn and Parley's life was spared.

ELDER Pratt raced his horse for about a mile through the forest and then found that the woods began to run out. Rather than expose himself in open country, he plunged back into the forest to await the darkness of night. Parley recorded:

74

I then dismounted, tied my horse in a thicket, walked some distance from him and climbed a tree — intending to wait in this situation amid the concealment of the thick foliage till the darkness of evening would enable me to proceed with safety. Seating myself in one of its forked branches, and placing my arms in two other similar forks, I was supported from falling, although in a moment after I had ceased my exertions I fainted away [Parley had been very ill]. In this situation I remained for some time, without the least power to change my position or help myself; my breath was gone through exertion, and my mouth and throat parched with a burning thirst, my stomach sickened . . .[45]

When he awoke, he found that his horse had gotten loose and was not seen again. However, thrilled with the joys of freedom, Parley exclaimed aloud, "Thank God for this hour, it is the happiest of my life; I am free, although lost in the wilderness, and if I cannot find myself, thank God nobody else can find me."[46] Elder Pratt was then successful in making his way to Illinois.

ORSON Pratt and Brother Clark were almost trapped, but slipping into a brush covered ravine, and lying there motionless, they managed to escape after dark. King Follet was recaptured and put back in prison until released several months later. Morris Phelps made good his escape, although he narrowly missed being taken again. While riding toward Illinois, he was suddenly surrounded in the darkness by a company of horsemen who were out looking for the prisoners. Not knowing who he was, the horsemen hailed him in a determined tone and demanded that he identify himself. Phelps replied in such a rough and careless manner the men were convinced that he was not a man fleeing for his life, let alone a Mormon. After begging his pardon for accosting him in such a rough way, they let him continue his journey. He soon made his way to the Mississippi River and crossed into Illinois.[47]

IT has been estimated that between eight and ten thousand Saints were driven from the State of Missouri during the winter and spring of 1838-39.[48] With the apostasy of Elder Thomas B. Marsh and the death of David W. Patten, Brigham Young had become the senior member of the Quorum of the Twelve Apostles. On his broad shoulders fell much of the responsibility for seeing that the Church membership was prepared to leave Missouri. At a meeting of the brethren, called at Far West on January 29, 1839, additional plans were made. Brigham Young presented the motion that they enter into a covenant to stand by and assist the Saints in removing from the state. The resolve was carried and the following covenant prepared and signed by three hundred and eighty men:

> We, whose names are hereunder written, do for ourselves individually hereby covenant to stand by and assist one another, to the utmost of our abilities, in removing from this state in compliance with the authority of the state; and we do hereby acknowledge ourselves firmly bound to the extent of all our available property, to be disposed of by a committee who shall be appointed for the purpose of providing means for the removing from this state of the poor and destitute who shall be considered worthy, till there shall not be one left who desires to remove from the state . . .[49]

A committee of seven men was called to carry out the business of removal. Those named were William Huntington, Charles Bird, Alanson Ripley, Theodore Turley, Daniel Shearer, Shadrach Roundy and Jonathan H. Hale. It was their duty to see that the terms of the covenant were observed.

ILLUSTRATIVE of the thousands who were thus forced to flee Missouri for a refuge in Illinois, was the John Hammer family. Speaking of their condition, John said:

> Well do I remember the sufferings and cruelties of those days . . . . Our family had one wagon, and one blind horse was all we possessed towards a a team, and that one blind horse had to transport our effects to the State of Illinois. We traded our wagon with a brother who had two horses, for a light one horse wagon, thus accommodating both parties. Into this small wagon we placed our clothes, bedding, some corn meal and what scanty provisions we could muster, and started out into the cold and frost to travel on foot, to eat and sleep by the wayside with the canopy of heaven for a covering. But the biting frosts of those nights and the piercing winds were less barbarous and pitiful than the demons in human form before whose fury we fled . . . .

When night approached we would hunt for a log or fallen tree and if lucky enough to find one we would build fires by the sides of it. Those who had blankets or bedding camped down near enough to enjoy the warmth of the fire, which was kept burning through the entire night. Our family, as well as many others, were almost bare-footed, and some had to wrap their feet in cloths in order to keep them from freezing and protect them from the sharp points of the frozen ground. This, at best, was very imperfect protection, and often the blood from our feet marked the frozen earth. My mother and sister were the only members of our family who had shoes, and these became worn out and almost useless before we reached the then hospitable shores of Illinois. [50]

WITH her husband in prison, Mary Ann, the wife of Parley P. Pratt, was under the necessity of making arrangements for her and her children to leave Missouri. Fortunately, David Rogers assisted them in getting to Quincy, Illinois. Enroute, Sister Pratt almost lost a six year old daughter during a river crossing. In recording the incident, Parley said:

On crossing a swollen stream, Mrs. Pratt had left the carriage to cross on a foot bridge, leaving the children to ride through it. She had just crossed over and turned to look back, to see whether the carriage came through in safety, when she discovered a little girl's bonnet floating down the stream, and, on examination, as the carriage rose the bank, her daughter, a girl of six years old was missing from the carriage. The next moment she saw her floating down the swift current. She gave the alarm to Mr. Rogers, the driver, who instantly dropped the reins and sprang after her into the stream.

At this instant the horses, being high spirited and active, began to run, and would probably have dashed themselves and the carriage, goods, and the other child to pieces but for the timely interference of a large prong of a tree, which caught the carriage with such a strong hold that all was brought to a stand. In the meantime Mr. Rogers succeeded in rescuing the child and bringing her safe to shore.

She had, as she stated, pitched head foremost out of the carriage into the water. One of the wheels ran over her, and crushed her fast into the mud at the bottom of the stream; but as it rolled over she caught the spokes with her hands, and by this means the same weight that crushed her down brought her to the surface and saved her life. On examination the marks of the wheel were distinctly seen on both her thighs, which were seriously injured and nearly broken.[51]

A S the month of April, 1839, arrived, the exiled Saints became concerned about the fulfillment of a revelation given at Far West the previous year. On July 8, 1838, the Lord, through his servant Joseph, said:

> And next spring [spring of 1839] let them [the Twelve] depart to go over the great waters, and there promulgate my gospel, the fulness thereof, and bear record of my name.
>
> Let them take leave of my saints in the city of Far West, on the twenty-sixth day of April next, on the building-spot of my house, saith the Lord.
>
> Let my servant John Taylor, and also my servant John E. Page, and also my servant Wilford Woodruff, and also my servant Willard Richards, be appointed to fill the places of those who have fallen, and be officially notified of their appointment.[52]

At the time this revelation was received, the Saints were well established in Far West. The community was growing by leaps and bounds. There was no indication that the Twelve would have any major difficulty meeting the requirements of the Lord on the following April. However, what a difference the happenings of one year can make. During that period, the Saints had lost many of their leaders to prisons and the membership of the Church had been expelled from the state. Only a handful of Saints remained in Far West and they were making last minute arrangements for departure. Their every movement was closely watched by the mob.

THEODORE Turley was one of the few Saints still residing at Far West in the forepart of April 1839. As a member of the committee on removal, he was concerned with the final handling of Church properties and seeing the last Saints off for Illinois. On April 4, eight men came into the office of the committee on removal, namely: Captain Samuel Bogart, Dr. Laffity, John Whitmer, and five others. They presented Brother Turley with a paper containing the revelation of July 8, 1838, and asked him to read it. Turley replied:

> "Gentlemen, I am well acquainted with it." They said, "Then you, as a rational man, will give up Joseph Smith's being a prophet and an inspired man? He and the Twelve are now scattered all over creation; let them come here if they dare; if they do, they will be murdered. As that revelation cannot be fulfilled, you will now give up your faith."
>
> Turley jumped up and said, "In the name of God that revelation will be fulfilled." They laughed him to scorn. John Whitmer hung his head. They said, "If they (the Twelve) come, they will get murdered; they dare not come to take their leave here; that is like all the rest of Joe Smith's - - - - - prophecies."[53]

LITTLE did the mob know the type of men they were dealing with in the Twelve, and even less of Him who said: "Heaven and earth shall pass away, but my word shall not pass away." Brigham Young talked to those Apostles who were with him in Quincy, Illinois, about the revelation. "I asked them, individually, what their feelings were upon the subject. They all expressed their desires to fulfill the revelation. I told them the Lord God had spoken, and it was our duty to obey and to leave the event in his hands and he would protect us."[54]

ON April 18th, Brigham Young, Orson Pratt, Wilford Woodruff, John Taylor, George A. Smith and Alpheus Cutler left the safety of Quincy and made their way toward Far West, Missouri. As they traveled, the company met Elder John E. Page, who had just turned his wagon upside down and was in the process of scooping up a barrel of soft soap with his hands. Brigham related:

I told him I wanted him to go to Far West with us. He replied, he did not see that he could, as he had his family to take to Quincy. I told him his family would get along well enough, and I desired him to go up with us. He asked how much time I would give him to get ready. I answered, five minutes. We assisted in loading his wagon; he drove down the hill and camped, and returned with us. We travelled 30 miles and camped for the night. [55]

ELDERS Heber C. Kimball and Shadrach Roundy also arrived in the vicinity of Far West from a different direction. Heber secretly moved around the countryside and notified the brothers and sisters still in the neighborhood of the appointed time for the meeting. Just after midnight on April 26, 1839, the Saints assembled at the home of Brother Samuel Clark, and then proceeded to the building spot of the Lord's House. Brother Kimball remembered the evening as being a clear, moonlight night. He further recalled:

   . . . after singing, we recommenced laying the foundation, agreeable to the revelation given July 8th, 1838, by rolling a stone, upwards of a ton weight, upon or near the south-east corner.

   In company with Brother Brigham Young, we ordained Wilford Woodruff and George A. Smith (who had been previously nominated by the First Presidency, accepted by the Twelve, and acknowledged by the Church at Quincy) members of the quorum of the Twelve Apostles; and Darwin Chase and Norman Shearer, (who was liberated from Richmond prison on the 24th inst, where they had been confined about six months for the cause of Christ) Seventies. They sat on the south-east corner stone while we ordained them.

   The Twelve then individually called upon the Lord in prayer, kneeling on the corner stone; after which "Adam-ondi-Ahman" was sung.[56]

AS the brethren were leaving Far West, Theodore Turley thought of his old friend, Isaac Russell, whose home they were then passing. Russell had renounced the Church and become an apostate. Turning to Elders Page and Woodruff, Brother Turley said:

"Stop a bit, while I bid Isaac Russell good bye;" and knocking at the door, called Brother Russell. His wife answered, "Come in, it is Brother Turley." Russell replied, "It is not; he left here two weeks ago;" and appeared quite alarmed; but on finding it was Brother Turley, asked him to sit down; but the latter replied, "I cannot, I shall lose my company." Who is your company?" enquired Russell. "The Twelve." "The Twelve!" "Yes, don't you know that this is the twenty-sixth, and the day the Twelve were to take leave of their friends on the foundation of the Lord's House, to go to the islands of the sea? The revelation is now fulfilled, and I am going with them." Russell was speechless, and Turley bid him farewell. [57]

The terms of the revelation which the mob said could not be fulfilled had been successfully complied with. Before sunrise the brethren departed the area. Brigham Young recorded, "We rode 32 miles and camped at the Tenney's Grove for the night. We learned that a mob had collected in different places, and on their arrival in Far West they found out we had been there and transacted our business." [58]

ALTHOUGH the exiled Saints went into several Illinois counties, Adams county became the primary gathering place during those first months. A majority of those forced out of Missouri crossed the Mississippi River at Quincy and located in the area. Brigham Young advised the Saints to "Settle, if possible, in companies, or in such a way that they could be organized into branches, so that they might be 'fed by the shepherds; for without, the sheep would be scattered.'"[59] On March 18, 1839, Brigham had met with several of the Twelve Apostles and advised them all to locate their families in Quincy, county seat of Adams County, "that we might be together in council."[60] The Saints had been stripped of nearly all their earthly possessions and were in a sad condition when they reached Quincy. Their desperate situation soon excited the sympathy of the residents of that community. As a result, they were given a kindly reception.

THE Prophet Joseph arrived in Quincy on April 22, suffering from fatigue and hunger, but cheered, as he declared, by "the congratulations of my friends, and the embraces of my family."[61] Wilford Woodruff just returning from Far West, has expressed his innermost feelings as he first met with Joseph following the prophet's lengthy imprisonment:

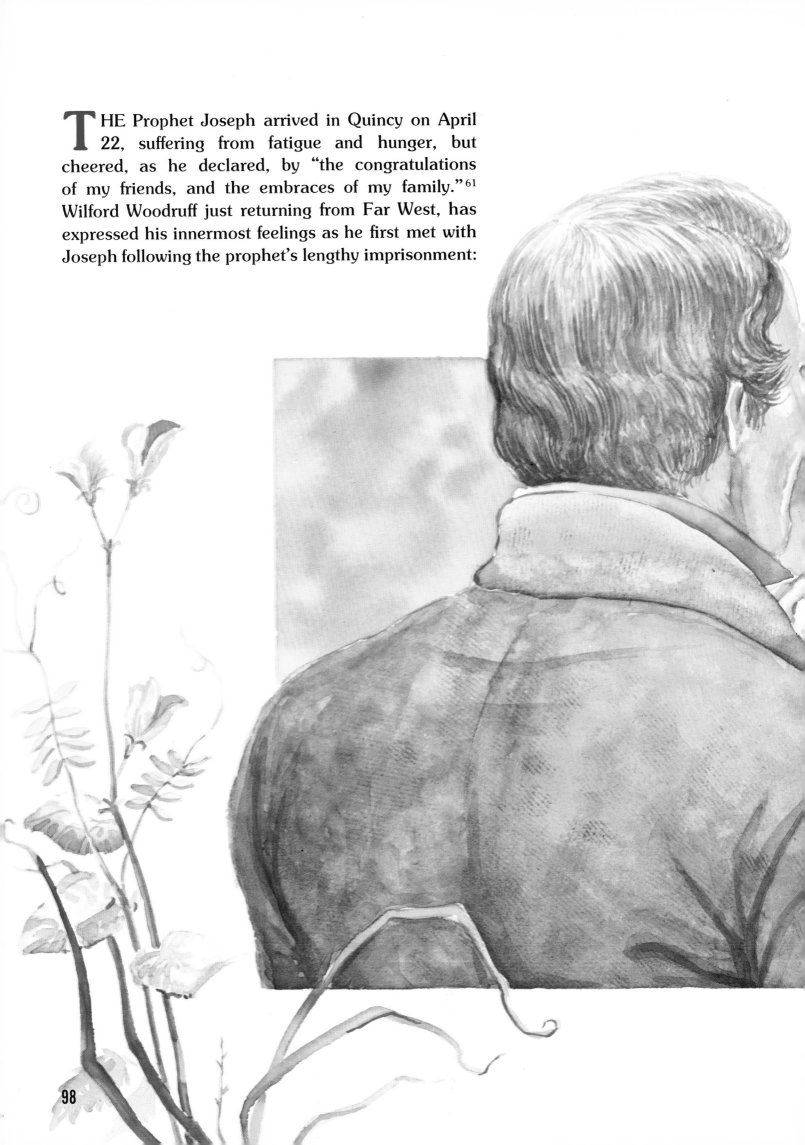

In company with five others of the quorum of the Twelve, I rode to Mr. Cleveland's, four miles out of town, to visit Brother Joseph Smith and his family. Once more I had the happy privilege of taking Brother Joseph by the hand. Two years had rolled away since I had seen his face. He greeted us with great joy, as did Hyrum Smith and Lyman Wight, all of whom had escaped together from their imprisonment. They had been confined in prison six months, and had been under sentence of death three times; yet their lives were in the hands of God. He delivered them, and now they were mingling with their wives, children, and friends, out of the reach of the mob. Joseph was frank, open, and familiar as usual, and our rejoicing was great. No man can understand the joyful sensations created by such a meeting, except one who has been in tribulation for the gospel's sake.[62]

ALMOST immediately upon his arrival in Quincy, Joseph went into council with the brethren regarding a suitable location for the Saints. It was agreed that the Prophet should investigate lands in both Iowa Territory and the state of Illinois. On April 25th Joseph and a select committee, visited properties owned by Isaac Galland in Lee County, Iowa. Pleased with what they saw, the committee later that year purchased the town of Nashville and 20,000 adjoining acres in Iowa. [63] Joseph and his party next visited Hancock County, Illinois, and on May 1, according to the Prophet:

> "purchased, in connection with others of the committee, a farm of Hugh White, consisting of one hundred and thirty-five acres, for the sum of five thousand dollars; also a farm of Dr. Isaac Galland, lying west of the White purchase, for the sum of nine thousand dollars . . . ."[64]

Payments on these lands were to come from (1) monies held by the Saints, (2) land changes in Missouri, and (3) periodic installments. Other land purchases were subsequently made.

ANXIOUS to find a permanent home, Joseph and his family moved to the site of the White purchase and took up his residence in a small log house on the bank of the river, about one mile south of the city of Commerce, Illinois. Hundreds of others also began to locate in the area, on both sides of the Mississippi River. The Prophet described his new surroundings in these words:

When I made the purchase of White and Galland, there were one stone house, three frame houses, and two block houses, which constituted the whole city of Commerce. Between Commerce and Mr. Davidson Hibbard's, there was one stone house and three log houses, including the one that I live in, and these were all the houses in this vicinity, and the place was literally a wilderness. The land was mostly covered with trees and bushes, and much of it so wet that it was with the utmost difficulty a footman could get through, and totally impossible for teams. Commerce was so unhealthful, very few could live there; but believing that it might become a healthful place by the blessing of heaven to the Saints, and no more eligible place presenting itself, I considered it wisdom to make an attempt to build up a city. [65]

JOSEPH later named the place "Nauvoo" a word which comes from the Hebrew signifying a beautiful location and "carrying with it also," said Joseph, "the idea of rest." [66] The following description portrays its geographical situation on the Mississippi:

The site of the city of Nauvoo was directly across the river from Montrose, Iowa, about 12 miles by the river north of Keokuk, 15 miles from Warsaw, Illinois, 53 from Quincy, and 191 from St. Louis. There is at that point a bend in the river that makes a long smooth arc pointing toward the west and leaving a big bulge of bottom land on the Illinois side jetting into Iowa. Since the river flows by on the north, west, and south, the bulge is a kind of peninsula shaped like a half-elipse, two miles long from north to south and a mile wide. A line of broken bluffs runs north and south along the east or land side of the peninsula, meeting the river on the north at the beginning of its bend and again on the south at the completion of the bend. The peninsula, which is low and flat, is separated by the bluffs from the higher prairie which stretches eastward from their top. The peninsula, the bluffs, and a considerable area on the adjacent prairie were all to be included in the City of Nauvoo. [67]

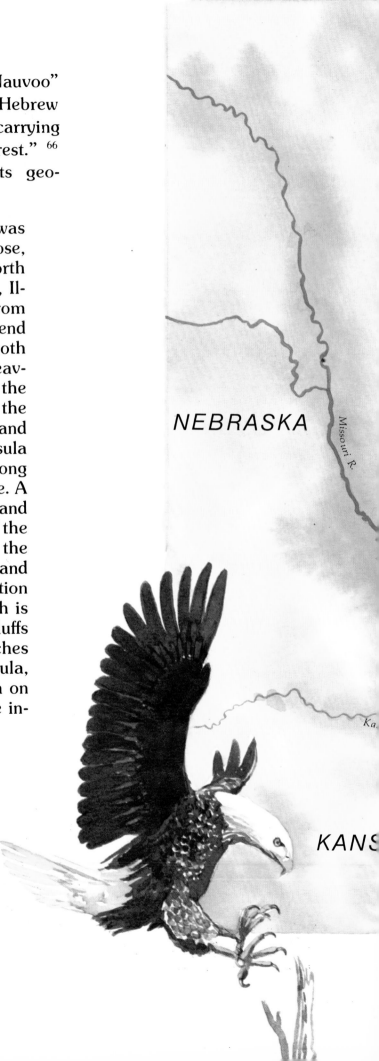

NEBRASKA

Missouri R.

Ka.

KANS

104

WISCONSIN

IOWA

ILLINOIS

MISSOURI

Cedar

Noda way

Des Moines R.

Skunk

Mississippi R.

Illinois R.

Platte

Grand R.

Thompson

Weldon

Locust Cr.

Chariton

Crooked Cr.

Salt

FT. MADISON

MONTROSE   NAUVOO
                CARTHAGE

KEOKUK

WARSAW

QUINCY

HANNIBAL

ADAM-ONDI-
AHMAN

GALLATIN   MILLPORT

FAR
WEST

HAUNS
MILL

DEWITT

LIBERTY   RICHMOND

ORTH

INDEPENDENCE

ST. LOUIS

Joseph Smith's log house in Nauvoo.

THE unhealthful nature of the swamp was eventually changed by the introduction of drainage ditches along the base of the bluffs. However, this was not accomplished before malaria and other disorders associated with the dampness of the peninsula took their toll. The Saints, weakened by their past situation, fell easy prey to sickness. Members of the Church were flocking into the community and, having no homes, were living in wagons, tents and on the ground. In this condition, many became sick through exposure. The Prophet gave up his own home to the sick and pitched a tent in his dooryard. He was almost completely worn out from waiting on those who were so ill about him. Elder Wilford Woodruff has recorded what proved to be one of the most miraculous series of healings ever recorded—truly a "day of miracles:"

On the morning of the 22nd of July, 1839 he Joseph arose, reflecting upon the situation of the Saints of God in their persecutions and afflictions. He called upon the Lord in prayer, the power of God rested upon him mightily, and as Jesus healed all the sick around Him in His day, so Joseph, the Prophet of God, healed all around on this occasion. He healed all in his house and dooryard; then, in company with Sidney Rigdon and several of the Twelve, went among the sick lying on the bank of the river, where he commanded them in a loud voice, in the name of Jesus Christ, to rise and be made whole, and they were all healed. When he had healed all on the east side of the river that were sick, he and his companions crossed the Mississippi River in a ferry-boat to the west side, where we were, at Montrose. The first house they went into was President Brigham Young's. He was sick on his bed at the time. The Prophet went into his house and healed him, and they all came out together. [68]

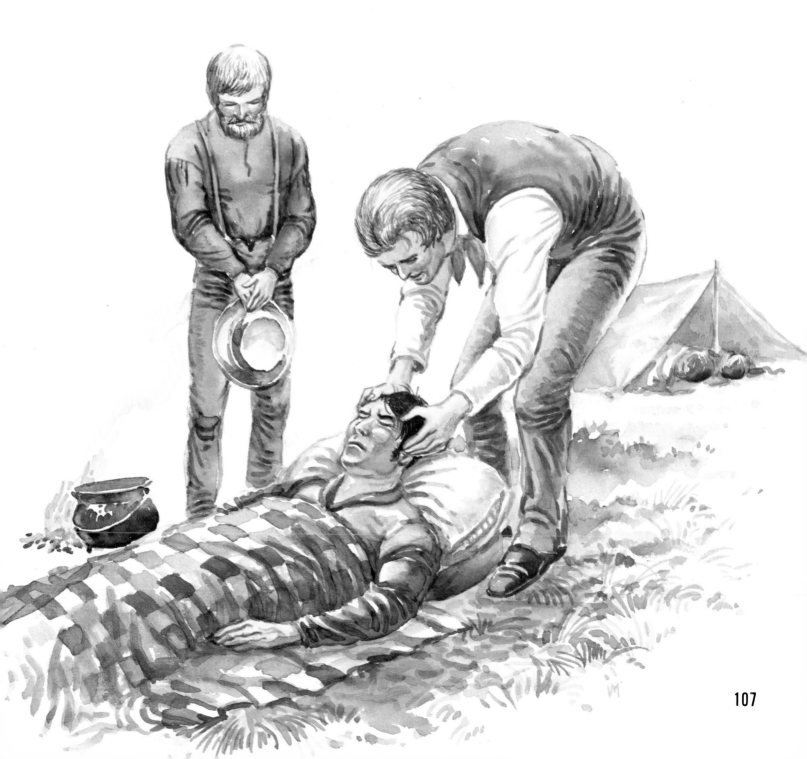

PASSING Brother Woodruff's door, the Prophet said: "Brother Woodruff, follow me." He then crossed the public square and entered Brother Elijah Fordham's house. Brother Fordham was close to death, eyes glazed, and unconscious. Elder Woodruff further explained:

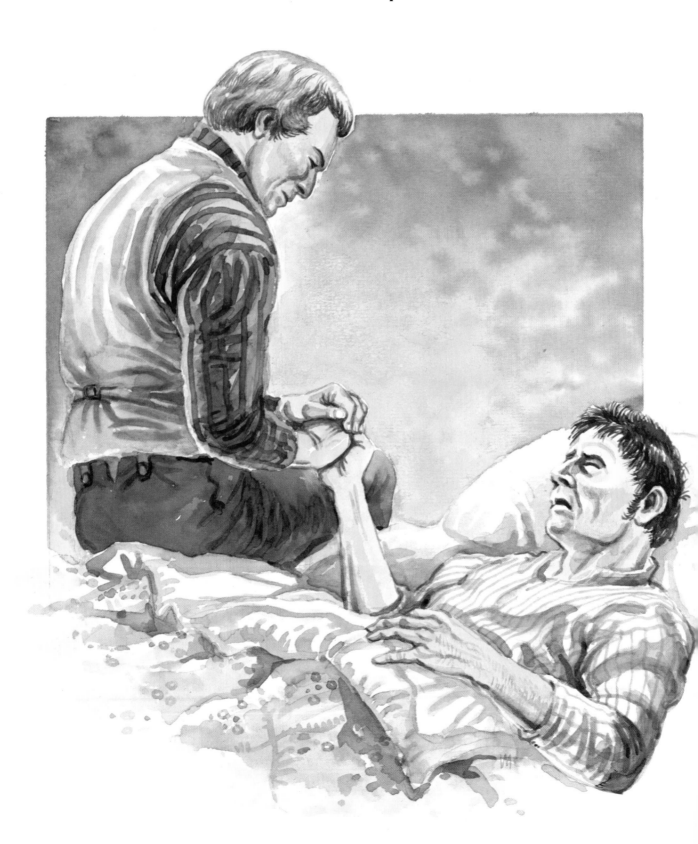

After taking his hand, he Joseph looked down into the dying man's face and said: "Brother Fordham, do you not know me?" At first there was no reply, but we all could see the effect of the spirit of God resting on the afflicted man. Joseph again spoke. "Elijah, do you know me?" With a low whisper Brother Fordham answered, "Yes." The Prophet then said: "Have you not faith to be healed?" The answer, which was a little plainer than before, was: "I am afraid it is too late; if you had come sooner, I think I might have been." He had the appearance of a man waking from sleep; it was the sleep of death. Joseph then said: "Do you believe that Jesus is the Christ?" "I do, Brother Joseph," was the response. Then the Prophet of God spoke with a loud voice, as in the majesty of Jehovah; "Elijah, I command you, in the name of Jesus of Nazarath, to arise and be made whole."

The words of the Prophet were not like the words of man, but like the voice of God. It seemed to me that the house shook on its foundation. Elijah Fordham leaped from his bed like a man raised from the dead. A healthy color came to his face, and life was manifested in every act. His feet had been done up in Indian meal poultices; he kicked these off his feet, scattered the contents, then called for his clothes and put them on. He asked for a bowl of bread and milk, and ate it. He then put on his hat and followed us into the street, to visit others who were sick. [69]

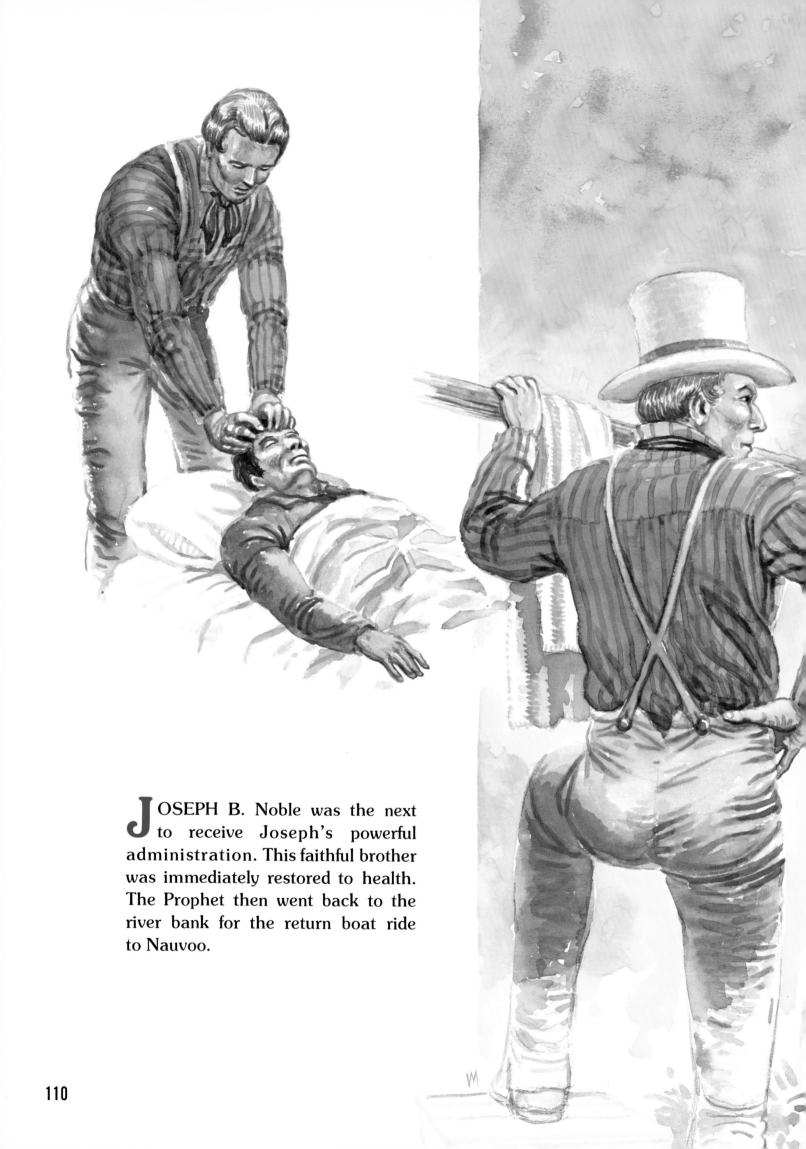

JOSEPH B. Noble was the next to receive Joseph's powerful administration. This faithful brother was immediately restored to health. The Prophet then went back to the river bank for the return boat ride to Nauvoo.

As he waited for the ferry, a non-Mormon gentleman stepped up to Joseph and asked him if he would come and heal his twin children who were just five months of age and very close to death. The infants were some two miles from there. Unable to go at that time, the Prophet said that he could not, but would send someone to attend them. Turning to Brother Woodruff he declared, "You go with the man and heal his children." Joseph then gave some unusual directions to Wilford. Elder Woodruff reported:

He took a red silk handkerchief out of his pocket, gave it to me, told me to wipe their faces with the handkerchief when I administered to them, and they should be healed. He also said to me: "As long as you will keep that handkerchief, it shall remain a league between you and me." I went with the man, did as the Prophet commanded me, and the children were healed. I have possession of the handkerchief unto this day. [70]

111

IT isn't known just how many of the Saints lost their lives as a consequence of the persecutions experienced in Missouri. Some have estimated the loss to be close to three hundred.[71] This would include those who died in direct mob action and those who subsequently died as a result of privations suffered in the exodus. In Missouri, designing men had sought to destroy "Mormonism" through the imprisonment of its leaders and the willful scattering of the faithful membership. However, they were disappointed in this.

The Lord miraculously preserved the Saints and grasped His Prophet from the very jaws of death. Now, gathered in a new land, the modern children of Israel commenced to build a city and a temple where they might witness the "salvation of God" and watch for His "arm to be revealed."

FOOTNOTES

1 Judge Joseph Thorp, *Early Days in the West: Along the Missouri One Hundred Years Ago* (Liberty: Irving Gilmer, 1924), p. 88.

2 Ebenezer Robinson (ed.), *The Return, II* (January 1890), 206.

3 Orson F. Whitney, *Life of Heber C. Kimball* (Salt Lake City: The Juvenile Instructor Office, 1888), 288, hereafter cited as Whitney, *Life of Heber C. Kimball.*

4 Missouri State Department, *Document containing the Correspondence, orders, etc., in Relation to the Disturbances with the Mormons* (Fayette: Boon's Lick Democrat, 1841), p.70.

5 Joseph Smith, *History of The Church of Jesus Christ of Latter-day Saints,* ed. B.H. Roberts (2d ed. rev.: Salt Lake City: Deseret Book Co., 1964), vol. 3, p. 445, hereafter cited as *HC.*

6 Parley P. Pratt, *Autobiography of Parley Parker Pratt* (Salt Lake City: Deseret Book Company, 1938), pp. 186-187, hereafter cited as Parley P. Pratt, *Autobiography of Parley Parker Pratt.*

7 Leland Homer Gentry, "A History of the Latter-day Saints in Northern Missouri from 1836 to 1839" (unpublished Doctor's dissertation, Brigham Young University, 1965), p. 517, hereafter cited as Gentry, "A History of the Latter-day Saints in Northern Missouri."

8 Ibid., p. 518.

9 Ibid., p. 520.

10 George A. Smith, Address delivered in the Tabernacle, May 24, 1874, *Journal of Discourses,* reported by David W. Evans, XVII (Liverpool, England, 1875), p. 91.

11 Gentry, "A History of the Latter-day Saints in Northern Missouri," pp. 485-86.

12 Andrew Jenson, *Latter-day Saint Biographical Encyclopedia* (Salt Lake City: The Deseret News, 1901), vol. 1, pp. 280-81.

13 Whitney, *Life of Heber C. Kimball,* p. 229.

14 Ibid., p. 230.

15 *HC,* 3:193.

16 Lucy Mack Smith, *History of Joseph Smith* (Salt Lake City: Bookcraft, 1958), pp. 290-91.

17 Parley P. Pratt, *Autobiography of Parley Parker Pratt, p. 192.*

18 *HC,* 3:200-201.

19 P.P. Pratt, *History of the Late Persecution* Detroit: Dawson and Bates, 1839), pp. 47-48.

20 *HC,* 3:206.

21 Parley P. Pratt, *Autobiography of Parley Parker Pratt,* p. 211.

22 Ibid.

23 *HC,* 3:417.

24 U.S., Congress, Senate, *Document Showing the Testimony Given Before the Judge of the Fifth Judicial District of the State of Missouri, on the Trial of Joseph Smith, Jr., and others, for High Treason and other Crimes Against that State, 26th Congress, 2d Sess.,* (Washington: Government Printing Office), 1841, p. 1.

25 Parley P. Pratt, *Autobiography of Parley Parker Pratt,* p. 214.

26 *HC,* 3:420.

27 Lyman Omer Littlefield, *Reminiscences of Latter-day Saints* (Logan: Utah Journal Co., 1888), p. 80, hereafter cited as Littlefield, *Reminiscences of Latter-day Saints.*

28 Gentry, "A History of the Latter-day Saints in Northern Missouri," pp. 566-67.

29 *Times and Seasons* [Nauvoo], February 1840, p. 52.

30 *HC,* 3:257.

31 *The Saints' Herald* [Lamoni, Iowa] August 2, 1884, p. 490.

32 F. Mark McKiernan, *The Voice of One Crying in the Wilderness:* Sidney Rigdon, Religious Reformer, 1793-1876 (Kansas: Coronado Press, 1971), pp. 98-99.

33 *HC,* 3:257-58.

34 Ibid., 292.

35 The Doctine and Covenants (Salt Lake City: The Church of Jesus Christ of Latter-day Saints, 1954), 121:1-3, hereafter cited as D&C.

36 Ibid., 121: 7-9.

37 *HC,* 3:309.

38 Ibid., 3:314-15.

39 Ibid., 3:316.

40 Ibid., 3:423.

41 Parley P. Pratt, *Autobiography of Parley Parker Pratt,* p. 241.

42 Ibid., p. 245-46.

43 Ibid., p. 250.

44 Ibid., pp. 250-51.

45 Ibid., p. 253.

46 Ibid., pp. 255-56.

47 Ibid., pp. 256-62.

48 Gentry, "A History of the Latter-day Saints in Northern Missouri," p. 634.

49 *HC,* 3:251-54, unfortunately, some of the signatures have been lost.

50 Littlefield, *Reminiscences of Latter-day Saints,* pp. 72-73.

51 Parley P. Pratt, *Autobiography of Parley Parker Pratt,* p. 242.

52 D&C, 118:4-6.

53 *HC,* 3:306-307.

54 *Millennial Star,* XXV (September 5, 1863), 567, hereafter cited as *MS.*

55 Ibid., 567-68.

56 Whitney, *Life of Heber C. Kimball,* pp. 264-265.

57 *HC,* 3:339-40.

58 *MS,* 25:584.

59 *Historical Record,* ed. Andrew Jenson (Salt Lake City: By the Author, 1889), vol. 8, p. 735, hereafter cited as Jenson, *Historical Record.*

60 *MS,* 25:567.

61 HC, 3:327.

62 Matthias F. Cowley, *Wilford Woodruff* (Salt Lake City: The Deseret News, 1909), p. 102, hereafter cited as Cowley, *Wilford Woodruff.*

63 *HC,* 3:378.

64 Ibid., 342.

65 Ibid., 375.

66 B.H. Roberts, *A Comprehensive History of The Church of Jesus Christ of Latter-day Saints* (Salt Lake City: Deseret News Press, 1930), 11; *HC*, 4:121.

67 Robert Bruce Flanders, *Nauvoo, Kingdom on the Mississippi* (Urbana: University of Illinois Press, 1965), p. 39.

68 Cowley, *Wilford Woodruff*, p. 104.

69 Ibid., p. 105.

70 Ibid., p. 106.

71 Jenson, *Historical Record*, VIII, 733.

PREVIEW OF VOLUME VII

Joseph and the Saints busily engaged themselves in the tremendous task of building the city of Nauvoo and sought to obtain a liberal charter for their new community from the State of Illinois. True to their covenant at Far West, Missouri, the Twelve Apostles left Illinois to perform highly successful missionary labors in England. At the appointed time, Elder Orson Hyde courageously fulfilled his assignment to dedicate the land of Palestine. Late in 1839, the Prophet led a delegation to Washington, D.C., and made an extended appeal to the President and Congress of the United States to right the unlawful and unjust treatment which the Saints had received in Missouri. During this period, officials in Missouri began a series of attempts to arrest Joseph and return him to that state for imprisonment. But by timely assistance, he was able to evade his persecutors. This era is singularly marked by the commencement of the beautiful Nauvoo Temple and the introduction of such important ordinances as baptism for the dead, the endowment and the eternity of the marriage covenant.